Do You Ever Feel...

Written by Sharlie Zinniger

Illustrated by Tiffany Cunliffe

Printed in the United States of America

ISBN 13: 978-0-578-50089-8

Published by Kindle Direct Publishing.

For more information please visit www.sharliezinniger.com

For my mom, who is always willing to laugh, scream, and cry with me.

~ S.Z.

To my four little loves, for continuing to challenge and motivate me everyday.

~ T.C.

Do you ever feel

ANGRY

like a bear
ready to roar?
POP!

Do you ever feel

SILLY

like a hyena laughing on the floor?

Do you ever feel

Scared

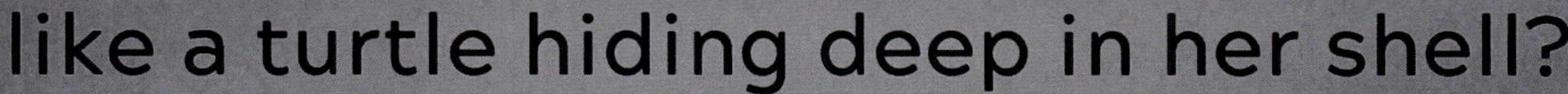

like a turtle hiding deep in her shell?

Do you ever feel

EMBARRASSED

like a monkey who slipped and fell?

Do you ever feel

like an elephant
under a sky of blue?

Do you ever feel

BORED

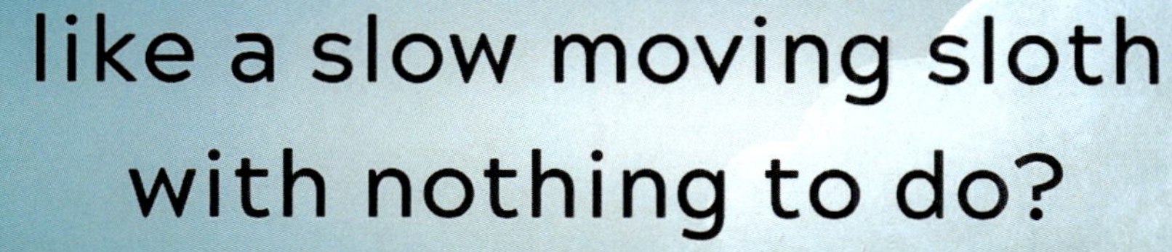

like a slow moving sloth
with nothing to do?

Nothing
to do...

Do you ever feel

LONELY

like a bird who doesn't belong to the flock?

Do you ever feel

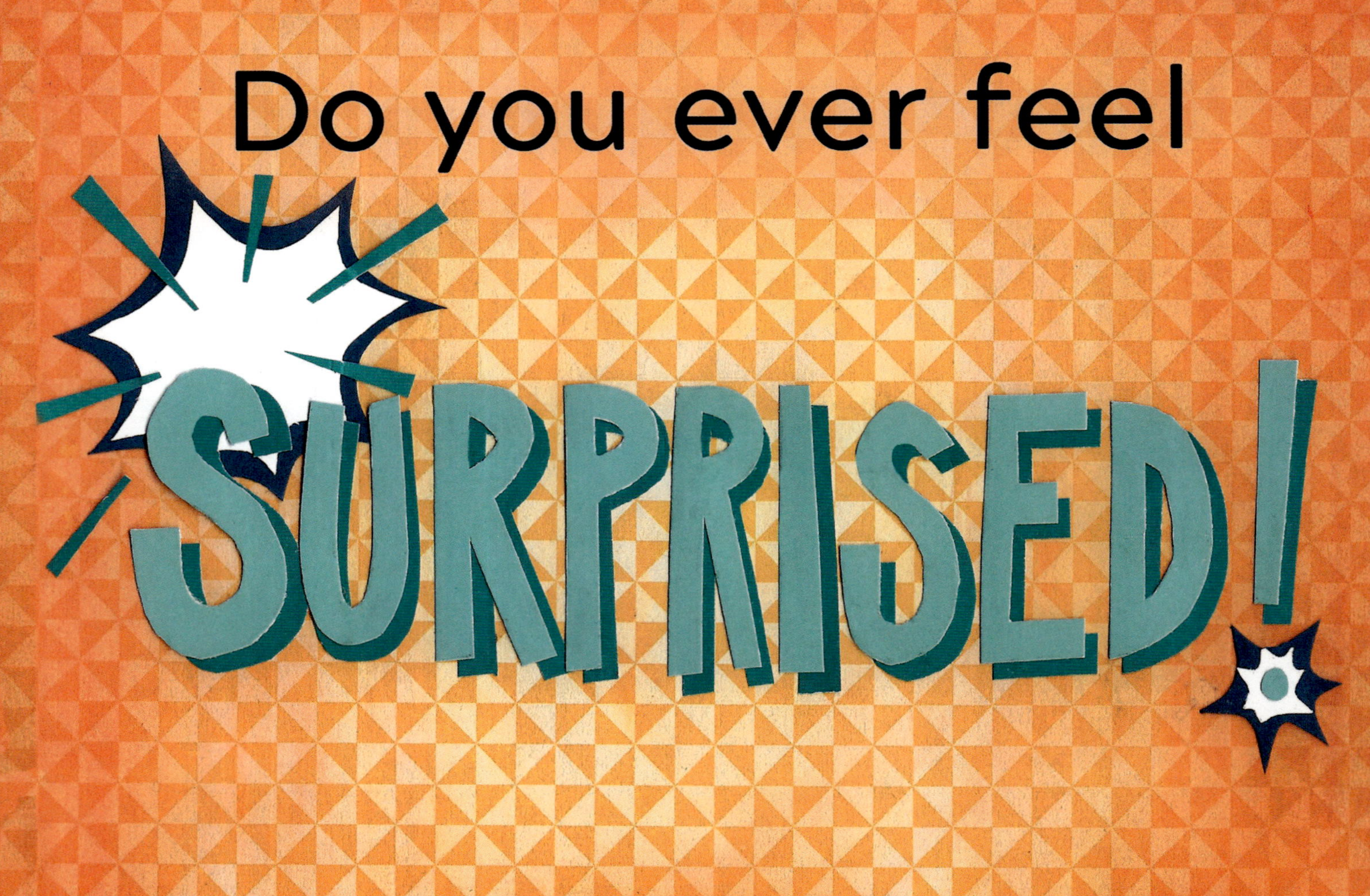

like a big-eyed owl when
he’s gotten a shock?

Do you ever feel

CONFIDENT

like a lion standing tall
in the pride land?

Do you ever feel

shy

like an ostrich who buries
her head in the sand?

Do you ever feel
sad

like a puppy
dog who misses
his friend?

Do you ever feel

confused

like a mouse in a maze
looking for the end?

Do you ever feel

NERVOUS

like a cat who is unsure of a new place?

Do you ever feel

excited!

like a seal with a treat
making this face?

It's OK to feel feelings-
whether silly or sad.

Everyone else feels them too,
I might add.

It's best to talk
about all that you feel.

Your feelings are part of you!
They are very, very real.

There will be times you feel
angry, happy, or shy.

You may want to
laugh, scream, or even cry.

No matter what you're feeling
how you act is up to you.

You can take a deep breath,
then choose what to do.

Your feelings may change as you go through the day.

Learn to recognize your feelings
and you'll be okay.

How Do You Feel?

Angry
Silly
Scared
Embarrassed
Happy
Bored
Confident
Surprised
Confused
Shy
Sad
Nervous
Excited
Lonely

shy ANGRY Scared
Happy NERVOUS
EMBARRASSED
BORED SURPRISED!
excited! sad LONELY
SILLY CONFIDENT
confused

Note to Parents and Caregivers,

After over 20 years working in the field of psychology, I have come to understand that emotional health is as important as physical health to quality of life. Emotional development begins from birth and unfolds throughout the lifespan. Books like this one are one tool to help children develop healthy emotional lives. As you read this book with your child, here are few things to keep in mind. First, avoid value judgments when discussing emotions. Children need to understand that emotions aren't "good" or "bad." The most important message for them to hear is that all emotions are okay to feel. The important thing is what we do with those emotions. Second, if as a parent you are unsure how to respond to your child's emotions - be empathetic. Think about how it might feel to be in their shoes and try to express that. Third, never discourage emotional expression. I cringe when I hear parents tell children to "stop crying" or "don't be mad." This leads to a stunting of emotional growth and a deeply engrained belief that they are "not okay" because they feel a certain way. Instead, praise the way they handle difficult emotions. If you get stuck, think about how it could be worse and praise them for not doing that. The sooner they can learn to tolerate difficult emotions, the easier their (and your) life will be. Enjoy this book with your child and here's to a healthy emotional life.

Frank D. Weber, Ph.D., ABPP
Associate Professor of Psychology
Brandman University

SHARLIE ZINNIGER is the author of *Yes, I'm Adopted!* She has a Bachelor's Degree in English Literature from UVU and continues to be a lover of the written word. She enjoys celebrating random holidays and spending time with her husband and four children. Find out more at www.sharliezinniger.com

TIFFANY CUNLIFFE is a former art teacher turned stay at home mom and illustrator. She has a Bachelor's Degree in Art Education from BYU. She and her husband have four children; together they share a passion for adoption, faith and family.

Made in the USA
Middletown, DE
23 February 2021